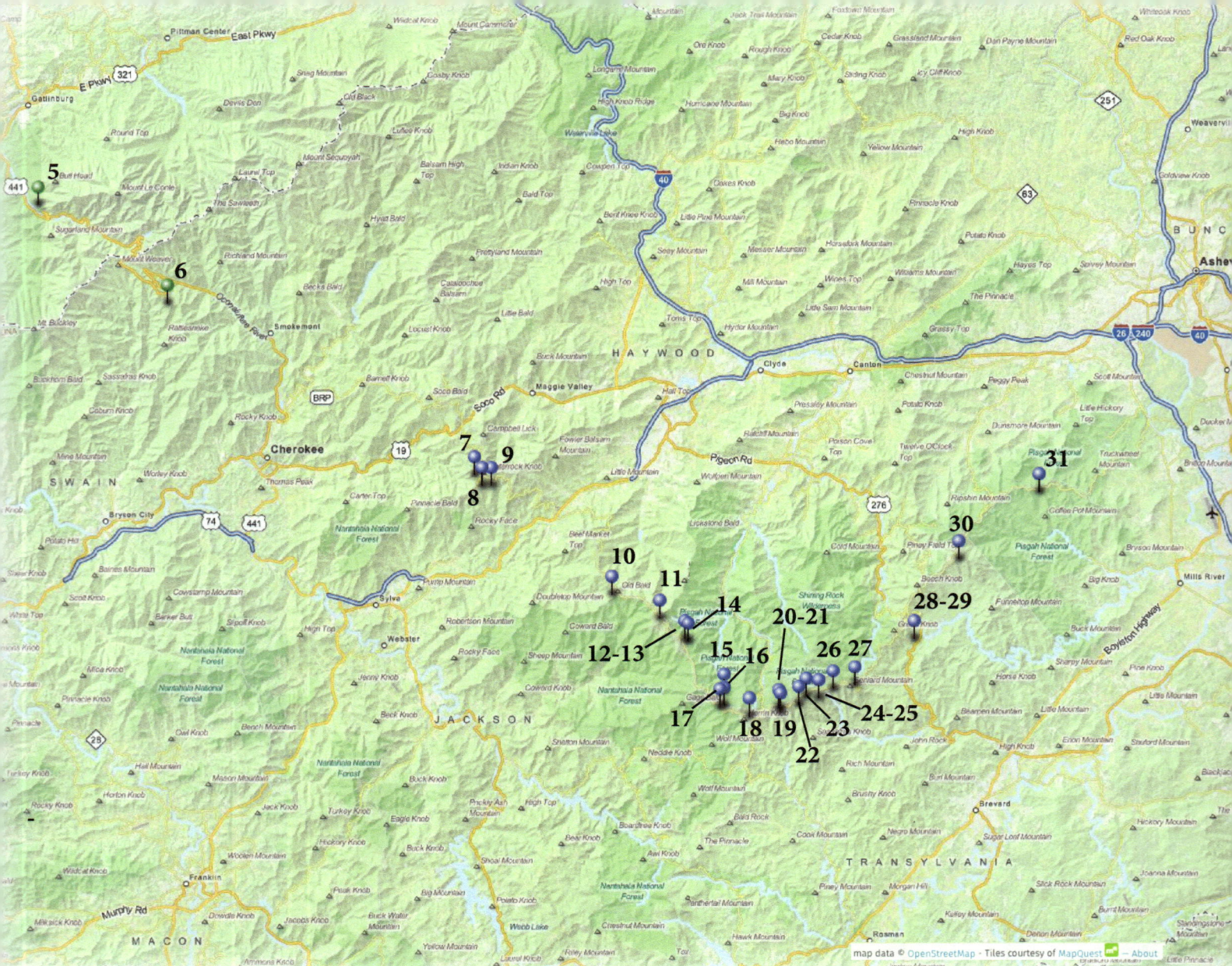

GREAT SMOKY MOUNTAINS TO ASHEVILLE

Driving the length of the Blue Ridge Parkway (and the scenic drives attached to it on each end), starts off with a bang in eastern Tennessee. The Great Smokies have quite a prominence, meaning how much of the mountain protrudes above the terrain around it. The Smokies rise aggressively from the Tennessee Valley to cloud and snow covered heights, and US 441 snakes its way to Newfound Gap at over 5,000' elevation.

As 441 becomes the start of the Blue Ridge, the Parkway crests near 6,000' again at the Plott Balsams, before quickly reaching its highest point at over 6,000' near Richland Balsam in the Great Balsam Mountains. After Mt. Pisgah, it is a tunnel-filled, winding descent into Asheville.

FOLLOWING PAGE:

US 441, on the Tennessee side of Great Smoky Mountain National Park, ascending toward Newfound Gap, looking east.

This section of the Parkway has the most forests similar to what is found in Canada out of the entire experience, an eerily serene passageway through the heavens. Waterfalls, national forests, and wilderness regions are in great abundance, through this section that is the highest average elevation of the entire drive.

For those who wish to see the most extreme nature with the least vestiges of human civilization, this is the section that I recommend, as one can literally get lost in the wilderness if they choose. Trails are in profound abundance, making it easy to get away from overlooks and well-trafficked picnic areas. Newfound Gap is stunning after a snowfall (4x4 may be required) and the Great Balsams are spectacular in the fall.

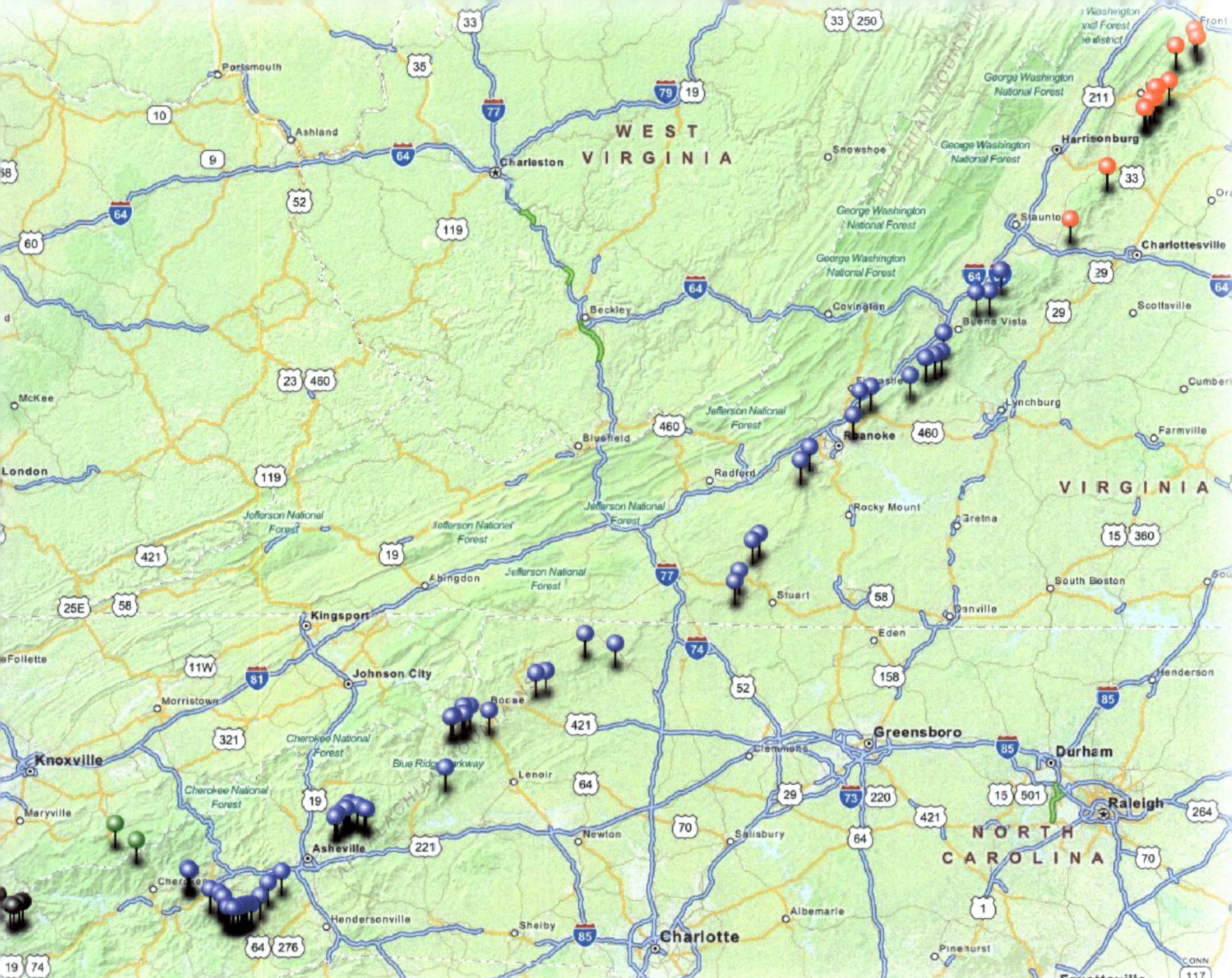

FLYING THE BLUE RIDGE PARKWAY

BLACK
Cherohala Skyway

GREEN
*US 441,
Great Smoky Mountains
National Park*

BLUE
Blue Ridge Parkway

RED
*Skyline Drive,
Shenandoah National Park*

Book, Text, and Photographs Copyright © 2015 Garrett Fisher. All rights reserved.

Maps Copyright © OpenStreetMap contributors. Map data, including map modifications made by the author, is available under the Open Database License, cartography licensed as CC-BY-SA. Please see openstreetmap.org, opendatacommons.org, and creativecommons.org.

ISBN: 0692408649
ISBN-13: 978-0692408643
Library of Congress Control Number: 2015904207

Published by Tenmile Publishing LLC - Alpine, WY
Website & Blog: garrettfisher.me

All photos in this book are available as prints, digital files, and framed prints. Please visit the website.

FRONT COVER: Craggy Gardens, Blue Ridge Parkway.   **REAR COVER:** Blue Ridge Parkway, Mile Marker 41, Virginia.

Table of Contents

Map of Photographs	1
Great Smoky Mountains National Park to Asheville	4 to 31
Introduction	8 to 14
To Fly the Blue Ridge	15 to 40
Asheville to Grandfather Mountain	32 to 51
Never Again: Tumble on the Ridge	50 to 91
Grandfather Mountain to Roanoke	52 to 67
Roanoke to Shenandoah National Park	68 to 81
Shenandoah National Park	82 to 97
Cherohala Skyway	98 to 103

> "When the engineers laid out the path of the Blue Ridge Parkway before the computer age, they left me wondering if they designed the Parkway to be viewed from an airplane."
> - Garrett Fisher

BACKGROUND: *BRP Mile Marker 352, with fog over the Piedmont, looking southeast.*

Above: *US 441, GSMNP, North Carolina side, looking west.* **Right:** *BRP MM 451, looking northwest.*

Introduction

I became aware of the Blue Ridge Parkway when I was in my teen years, after some retired relatives that migrate annually between NY and Florida decided to drive the length of the Parkway on the way back to New York. They spoke wistfully of this parkway "where it is spring in the valley, winter on the mountain, and spring in the valley again. It happens over and over as we drove the length of it." I was instantly hooked, and wanted to experience this phenomenon. I otherwise knew very little of the terrain in the South, except for the glorious view visible from I-77 descending into North Carolina from Virginia, visible during an annual pilgrimage from New York to Florida.

Fast forward the greater portion of a decade and I found myself driving in thick fog, ascending out of Waynesville, NC heading east, finally on the Blue Ridge Parkway for

Above:

BRP MM 450, Watterock Knob Visitors Center, looking west toward the Great Smokies.

the first time. Miles and miles we drove, in the fog, fog that did not exist down in civilization. Suddenly, we broke out of the fog bank, appearing above the clouds. Stopping at an overlook, I could see over 40 miles in clear late November air, an endless sea of mountains and clouds, and the bluest sky I had seen in the winter, having grown up in the Great Lakes. I loved every bit of it.

One year and a half later, I found myself living in Charlotte, North Carolina, and our first trip to the Blue Ridge Parkway was 2 weeks after arriving. Time and time again we drove to the mountains, more than I can recount, just in the first year. As the years went by, we visited some section of the Parkway every month to three months, eventually driving every single bit of it, including US 441 in the Great Smokies and Skyline Drive in Shenandoah National Park, save

for a few small sections closed for repairs. It quickly became a favorite for my wife and I.

As I sought new adventures, I climbed mountains and hiked waterfalls, all accessible from the Parkway, and did so in every single season, with a special emphasis on winter. Growing up with enormous piles of lake effect snow, the lack of winter in Charlotte resulted in many drives during extremely cold weather; chasing some form of view, warm coffee in hand, while most of the rest of the population was sitting by a fireplace. I made some flights over the Parkway in the earlier part of this decade, though gave no thought to anything other than a quick moment of recreation. There were many amusing events, including one drive to go to the top of Mt. Mitchell and hike to Mt. Craig in -2F weather, simply because I could, and the Parkway made it possible.

ABOVE:

BRP MM 449, Plott Balsams, looking north toward Maggie Valley.

FOLLOWING PAGE:

BRP MM 437, looking northeast toward Richland Balsam, the highest point on the Parkway.

Life eventually took us west, to the high terrain of the Rockies in Colorado. A year later, life took us back east to Charlotte. Having undertaken a massive book project in Colorado, photographing all 58 peaks over 14,000 feet from the airplane, I hatched a brilliant scheme to photograph my favorite things from the South, mostly from the airplane: the peaks over 6,000 feet in the Appalachians (there are 40), the Outer Banks, the wild horses in Corolla, and the Blue Ridge Parkway, each of which has their own book project.

The goal of the book is to show the essence of the Blue Ridge Parkway, end to end, including its sister parkways: US 441 in Great Smoky Mountains National Park, Cherohala Skyway in the southern corners of NC and TN, and Skyline Drive in Shenandoah National

ABOVE: *BRP MM 432, the highest point on the Parkway at the bottom of the image (6,047'), looking west.*

Park. Starting at Gatlinburg, TN and ending in Front Royal, VA, the book is a catalog of the most important sites of the entire journey, things that cannot be seen while on the ground. Each image is generally sequentially after the prior one, meaning that they proceed south to north as the page numbers increase in the book. For those who wish to savor the hikes and terrain visible from the images, maps and just enough detail is provided so the reader can do a simple internet search and figure out directions and hiking tips from the many guides available on the internet.

ABOVE:

BRP MM 430, passing beneath Reinhart Knob in the fog, looking west.

LEFT:

Author flying his Piper PA-11 aircraft, used in the production of this book. Photo: Adam Romer.

PAGES 12-13:

BRP MM 430, passing beneath Reinhart Knob (6,100'), looking west.

To Fly the Blue Ridge

Unlike some of the projects I have gotten myself into, flying over most of the Blue Ridge Parkway is a relatively benign prospect, something that is quite safe and enjoyable. At least, that is what I tell myself, and then I start thinking about the details, and realize that it is almost 500 miles of road, spanning the highest mountains in the Eastern United States, over quite a bit of terrain that makes its own weather. Then I reflect more so on some of the less pleasant flying events around the Blue Ridge Escarpment, and I realize that I should perhaps watch my words.

In *theory*, flying the Blue Ridge Parkway is a pleasant, easy project, given that there are breaks in the drama and intensity. When photographing the highest peaks of a region, there is the feeling that the intensity and danger is virtually nonstop, whereas the Blue Ridge has the illusion of providing periods of ease; therefore,

Above:

BRP MM 427, passing beneath Rough Butt Bald in autumn, looking southwest.

it *must be* safer overall. While it probably is, experience proves otherwise.

The challenge of undertaking the project is to capture the essence of the Parkway, the flowing road, gracefully sweeping and curving its way through any combination of rugged, soft, gentle, majestic, or quiet sections, doing so in an accurate yet artistically appealing way. Before speaking too much to that effect, the bigger concern is to successfully be able to pull off the flight, end to end, and be able to get close enough to have the photographs be worth looking at. I learned early on when mixing my camera with airplanes that any pilot can fly over almost any terrain, as long as it isn't so tall that the airplane can't get over it. One or two miles above "dangerous" terrain really isn't dangerous at all, as distance provides a safety buffer. The photographs aren't any good, as the dull two-dimensional images will

attest to. To get a good picture that provides accurate and compelling perspective, proximity becomes the necessity.

The obvious danger points have to do with the highest sections of the road. US 441 climbs through steep and aggressive terrain en route to Newfound Gap, cresting quite quickly at the low point of the pass at 5,049' elevation, walled in by Mt. Le Conte and Clingmans Dome, two very aggressive peaks. The Parkway then crests the Plott Balsams as it passes over roughly 5,720' elevation between Yellow Face and Watterock Knob. Next is the Great Balsam Mountains, where the highest point of the Parkway is found at 6,053' elevation, near Richland Balsam. After an extended period at high altitude, the Parkway heads down to Asheville for a respite, before heading back up to 5,840' near the entrance to Mt. Mitchell State Park. After this section, the Parkway stays well below 5,000', though passing by Grandfather Mountain closely (5,946'), and later skirting the Peaks of Otter, Apple Orchard Mountain, and Wintergreen Ski area, all at or near 4,000' elevation.

Terrain is the challenge, as it presents something physical to fly into, generally a result of bad weather interacting with the mountains. Speaking of which, these mountains create their own weather, with low clouds and fog a direct result of increased elevation. High-speed winds that would normally be just a minor annoyance become dangerous as they bend and twist over and around terrain, creating unpredictable air movements that require skill and experience to understand and avoid. There are many circumstances where the mountains create

ABOVE:

BRP MM 426, looking southwest, during autumn. Rough Butt Bald in the background.

RIGHT:

BRP MM 426, looking northeast, during low clouds and fog.

PAGE 18:

BRP MM 425 - Mt. Hardy Gap, looking west, during autumn.

ABOVE: *BRP MM 422, Devils Courthouse (bottom left), looking west toward NC 215 intersection with BRP.*

ABOVE: *BRP MM 421 - Chestnut Bald (6,020'), looking west.*

their own snow, rain, and thunderstorms, though that is not usually a problem on a day when photographs are being taken.

Aside from these issues, there is the ever-present concern of where to land if the engine were to fail. Most pilots that are cruising from one destination to another will cross rough terrain with plenty of altitude to spare, allowing a greater range of locations to make a forced landing. In a photography situation, the altitude buffer is smaller, so options are usually restricted to wilderness areas in the higher, rougher terrain. That meant that, in most instances, the Blue Ridge Parkway *itself* was my backup plan if the engine quit, trying to find a section without a curve, or a parking overlook to land the airplane aggressively if the worst were to happen. Thankfully, that never became a problem, and is a very

ABOVE:

BRP MM 420, access road to Black Balsam Knob and the Art Loeb Trail, looking northeast with low clouds.

PAGE 20-21:

BRP MM 422, Devils Courthouse, just along the Parkway. Image taken looking south with low clouds and fog.

PAGE 24-25:

BRP MM 420, Graveyard Fields, looking northeast during autumn.

rare instance with general aviation aircraft.

With the aforementioned list of concerns, one would think that the worst of the problems is over, and the rest is easy. I thought that entering the project, and discovered, for the second time, that the more dangerous situations have to do with high winds down at 3,000' above sea level, where the Blue Ridge Escarpment means the foothills. The chapter "Never Again" explains one near mishap during the production of the book, taking place near the NC/VA border, in one of the lowest, flattest sections of the entire Parkway.

After danger is out of the way, then it's a matter of how to capture the essence of the Parkway, its sweeping curves, views that extend great distances, aggressive terrain, and unique weather. The goal with

ABOVE: *BRP MM 419, looking west into fog.* **RIGHT:** *BRP MM 418, Graveyard Fields, looking west.*

ABOVE: *BRP MM 414, looking west toward the Great Balsam Mountains.*

ABOVE:

BRP MM 408, Mt. Pisgah, looking northwest, during autumn.

RIGHT:

BRP MM 404, ascent to Mt. Pisgah (in the clouds), looking southwest on a foggy summer day.

all of my books is to show the subject in a unique and informative way, yet not so foreign that the person cannot relate; I am trying to bring the aerial experience to the ground. Unlike my mountain books, the Parkway is a continuous entity, not a series of finite points to be documented. Therefore, I took care to try to show as much of the road as possible in each photograph, showing not only the curves and terrain, but also its progression through them, especially in areas where the view from the air was quite amazing. Sometimes, a photograph features very little of the road, and more of the terrain, as the Parkway is kind of "hanging" out over a steep section, and it is a place where an overlook is not possible. In a handful of occasions, the Parkway does not appear at all; rather, I show a main attraction alongside the Parkway that many visit when taking the drive. My favorite is to show repeated curves and turns, one after another, as it almost looks as though the engineers laid out the road specifically to be viewed from these angles, making the Blue Ridge Parkway itself be a work of art, not just the scenery it shows.

Setting up the actual shot involves crisscrossing the Parkway at 30 to 50 degree angles, so I can photograph out the door or window, showing the length of the road in one shot. As the terrain ascends and descends frequently, it is also a task of changing altitude to stay with the Parkway, and not find myself too high. For example, I obtained some shots near Grandfather Mountain in Linville, NC, then found myself thousands of feet above nearby Blowing Rock, NC, making those photos dull, requiring a 2,000' descent to get back on track. That all happened over a short distance. When it is all said and done, there is no formula as to what is a good photograph of the Parkway, as so much (continued page 35)

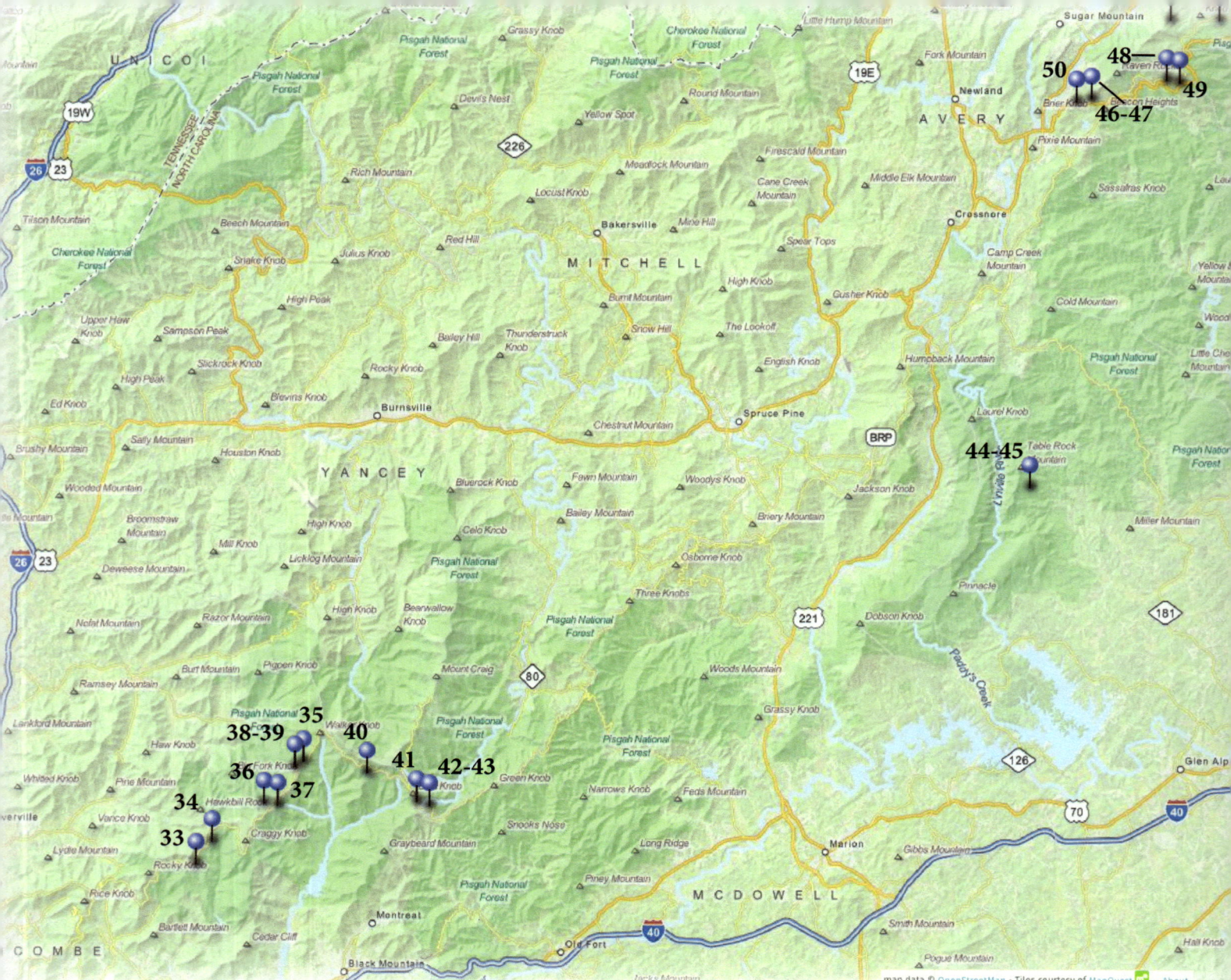

Asheville to Grandfather Mountain

This section is absolutely my favorite in the entire Southeast, not just of the Parkway. Containing the duality of both varied and aggressive terrain as well as the ability to live around such features, the region has a unique lifestyle, as well as access; other sections of the Parkway lack one of these key features.

Craggy Gardens is an interesting ridge, first encountered outside of Asheville, where the Parkway flirts again with 6,000' elevation. Trees are stunted, a product of harsh winds, creating a gnarly look to the vegetation, something different than the typical Canadian evergreen forests found at this altitude. Continuing past Craggy Gardens, the experience reminds me of being in the Rocky Mountains, with pine trees, rock features, clear mountain air, and cold weather. The Black Mountains are the next stop, containing the highest terrain in the eastern half of North America. Linville Gorge Wilderness Area, while down at 2,000' to 4,000' elevation, is such a profound scene that I recommend researching Table Rock, Wiseman's View, and Linville Falls. I could devote an entire book to that area. Finally, Grandfather Mountain is a destination in and of itself, a beautiful, massive mountain with incredible terrain, views, and beauty, with the Parkway passing on its eastern slopes, another feature so prolific in interest that I could do a whole project on it.

If you have time, this section of the Parkway deserves well more than a simple trip in the car. I suggest researching the abundance of sights to see around the Parkway.

Right:

BRP MM 369, looking northeast toward Craggy Gardens, en route on the ascent from Asheville to Mt. Mitchell.

(continued from page 30) of it changes, and there is so much to be shown. I found the process to be quite a challenge to sift through my work and determine what belonged in the book, as the "best" representation from above.

For a technical explanation of the factors going into flight planning, weather, camera equipment, and how I actually photograph in the air, please see my book *Appalachian Altitude: Flying the Highest Peaks in the South*. I go into great detail regarding all of these factors, and they apply similarly here, as the projects were similar and overlapped to some extent.

From an artistic and photography standpoint, the road presented a new angle. My goal in any project is to capture the essence of a location, through angle, perspective, and composition, conveying the depth and magnitude of a place in a single image. Mountains and other finite destinations make that easy by providing one particular point as the focus of the image. In the case of the Parkway, it was both easier and difficult to capture a road that is nearly 500 miles long. On one hand, the road is a moving item, in lieu of a single point. Sometimes the best perspective to capture the terrain and surroundings may leave the Parkway largely out of the image, or shrouded by trees and other obstacles. If the road is included properly, then it provides tremendous flow, angle, and perspective, all by itself. Being that that Parkway winds and curves countless times, it is impossible to pick an ideal time of day, as the road is pointing any number of directions, into the sun, away from the sun, into terrain shadows and the like. In

ABOVE:

BRP MM 360, looking southwest along Craggy Gardens, with low clouds forming off the ridgeline and moving east.

LEFT:

BRP MM 368, looking southwest toward Asheville, descending from Craggy Gardens.

that respect, the Parkway dictated its own terms, and capturing it became a partially passive exercise, waiting to see what it offered as I flew by to photograph it.

It is noteworthy that many of the images have fog and low clouds in them. While I consider the greatest beauty of the Carolinas to be clear air, blue skies, and stunning rime ice or autumn colors, I found that the real achievement was to capture the Parkway in its elusive state, one that happens up to a third of the time, depending on location: interactions with changing cloud forms. Anyone who frequents the Parkway enough times will find that the clouds do amazing things, changing rapidly, and also pulling off these feats of beauty in localized areas. I made a specific point to gamble as to the feasibility of even seeing the Parkway by flying up during low clouds and fog

Above:

BRP MM 365, Craggy Dome (6,100'), looking east, with the foothills and Piedmont visible in the distance, during autumn.

Right:

BRP MM 361, glorious curves in the Parkway along Craggy Gardens, looking northeast, in autumn.

Pages 38-39:

BRP MM 365, Craggy Gardens, looking north from Craggy Dome.

events. Note that my aircraft is not certified for instrument operations, meaning that I cannot fly through clouds under any circumstances. Even highly technical aircraft that are certified for such activities cannot do so within almost half a mile of terrain, so the chances of seeing the Parkway with all of its mysterious fog and cloud behavior was quite low. I consider those images to be the best out of the entire book.

From an experience standpoint, it was quite pleasant to fly the length of the Parkway. Flights of over 57 miles are considered "cross country" flights, and most of them are a point A to point B affair, where the sights and scenery is part of an overall trip. The Parkway, of course, is not drawn out in a straight line, and it was quite enjoyable to follow the contour of the Blue Ridge Escarpment, along with some of the

highest peaks in the South, for an extended period. Admittedly, I was downright amazed at how the Parkway looked from the air in some terrain. In other sections, I was rather surprised as to extended periods amongst farmlands and woods, going on for miles and miles in sections of the Blue Ridge Plateau in Virginia. One thing is for certain: the Parkway contains something for everyone, even pilots.

ABOVE:

BRP MM 357, looking northeast with Mt. Gibbes (6,540') and Potato Knob visible to the left.

RIGHT:

BRP MM 354, looking northwest toward Mt. Mitchell access road.

PAGES 42-43:

BRP MM 352, looking east above the clouds over the Piedmont.

LEFT:

Above the clouds over the Blue Ridge, looking at Mt. Mitchell.

44 **Above:** *BRP MM 315-318, Linville Gorge, with Table Rock (3,909') to the right, looking west.*

Pages 46-47: *BRP MM 300, Grandfather Mountain, looking northeast.*

Never Again: Tumble on the Ridge

Page 48:

BRP MM 299, Grandfather Mountain with BRP and US 221 running along slopes. Looking southwest.

Page 49:

BRP MM 299, slopes of Grandfather Mountain with BRP and US 221 during late summer, facing southwest, including Linne Cove Viaduct.

While I am almost constantly preaching that aviation is quite safe, and that non-pilots are emotionally feeble drama queens that overreact to minor aviation scares, sometimes things don't go as planned. One October afternoon while flying over the Blue Ridge Escarpment was one of those moments that went very wrong, and ended up as a memoir in an aviation magazine.

Unlike driving, pilots are constantly concerned with safety, learning, skill, and self-improvement. Drivers merely buy more crash resilient cars, whereas pilots try to learn how to crash less. Thus, there are sections in aviation magazines dedicated to the pilot community learning from its mistakes. This story made it into one of those sections.

The best comparison to driving that I can make with this story is to imagine that you're driving down a country road, go around a curve, hit ice, and start fishtailing back and forth, nearly going off (continued page 57)

Above:

BRP MM 300, elongated summit ridgeline of Grandfather Mountain, looking southwest to northeast.

Right:

BRP MM 300, elongated summit ridgeline of Grandfather Mountain, looking opposite of above: northeast to southwest, with the Black Mountains on the horizon.

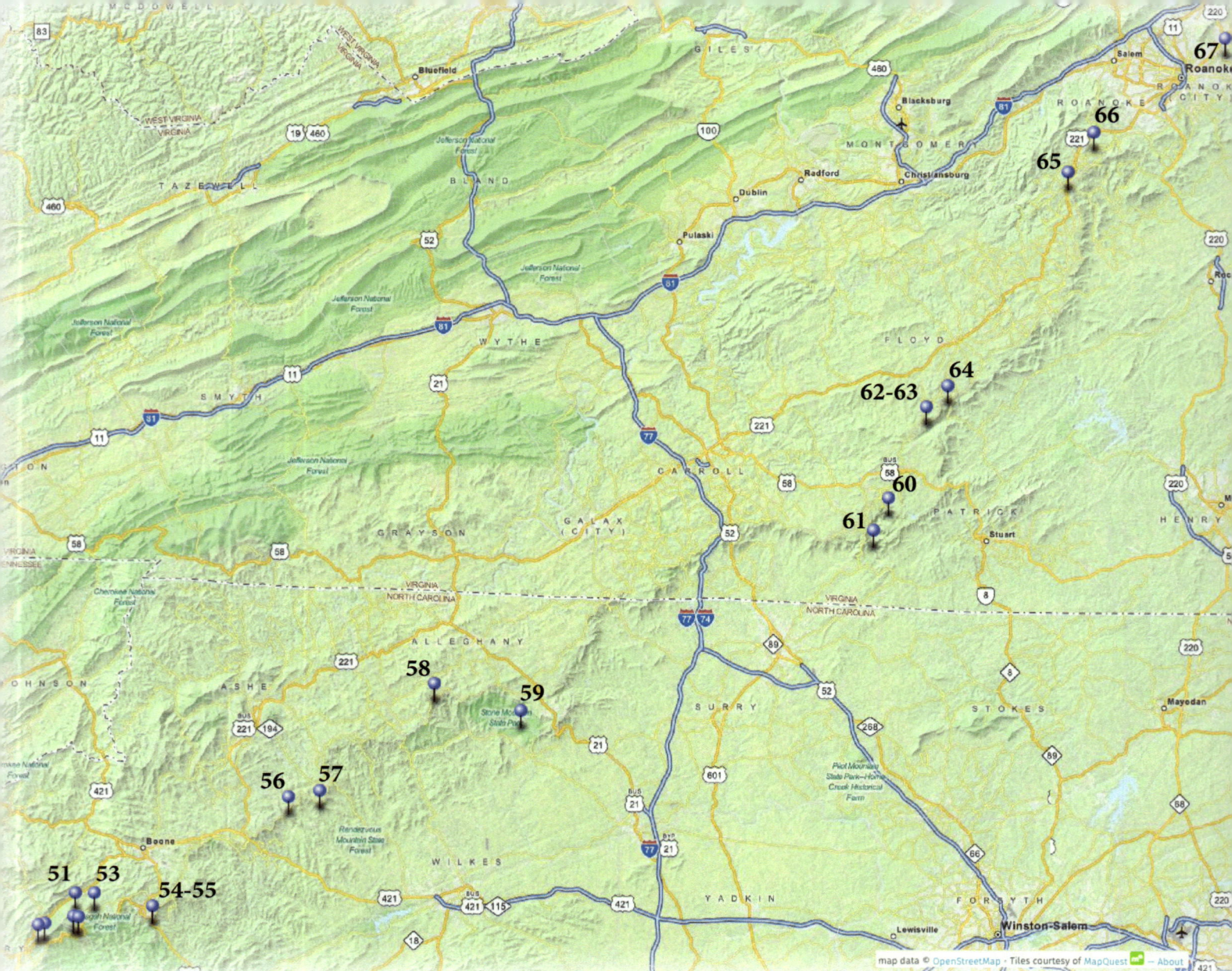

Grandfather Mountain to Roanoke

As the Blue Ridge descends off the slopes of Grandfather Mountain, it will not see such terrain severity until it reaches central Virginia, a significant distance away. En route, however, the Parkway takes on a different personality. Instead of majestic and severe, the scenery gives way to lakes, the picturesque village of Blowing Rock, Piedmont views, fields, Christmas tree farming, and rolling highlands.

Right:

BRP MM 296, Price Lake, just past Grandfather Mountain, looking northeast toward Blowing Rock.

Flying this section made a big difference in being able to appreciate another perspective not available on the ground: looking back into the Blue Ridge Plateau, seeing its pleasant beauty, something that is evident in some of the photographs, as they were taken from over the Piedmont looking northwest into the higher terrain.

Not to be unmatched is the fact that there were some surprises. The most outstanding was a canyon formed out of the Dan River as it descends down into the Piedmont below, a scene entirely unavailable from the Parkway. Other sights were quite interesting: mansions, a gothic cathedral, and forested terrain dropping rapidly into the Piedmont, examples which are suprisingly common in many places that I fly.

As a lover of extreme terrain, the airplane made up the difference as I traveled this section. Many miles pass under the canopy of forests, alongside farmlands, and without epic views, though they are adequately present at intervals. Sometimes the Parkway hides a visitor from a splendid view just over the hill.

ABOVE: *BRP MM 292, Blowing Rock NC, with "The Blowing Rock" in the bottom left, looking northwest.*

(continued from page 50) the road on both sides, only to end up back on the road, and the drive continues. Ultimately, no injury occurred, though the whole affair can be quite scary, and a person will try as much as possible to avoid repeating the incident. This is the aviation version of out–of–control fish tailing.

Originally Published in AOPA Pilot Magazine, P&E Never Again section, March 2015 issue.

Photo mission gone wrong

The flight was planned to be a photography exercise, documenting the terrain of the New River Basin in Virginia and West Virginia. The forecast called for sunshine, light westerly winds in North Car-

ABOVE:

BRP MM 265, "The Lump" at the base of the image, looking north into the Blue Ridge Plateau.

LEFT:

BRP MM 269, looking northwest into North Carolina Christmas Tree farming area.

olina, with a breezy day in the Virginias.

I set off from Lincoln County Regional Airport, outside of Charlotte, North Carolina, in my Piper PA–11 with a Continental O-200 engine. It is a simple aircraft with no electrical system. The route of flight was straight over the Brushy Mountains and north into the Blue Ridge Plateau in Virginia. The ascent itself into Virginia was uneventful, except the wind was absolutely howling with moderate turbulence in the higher terrain.

After 20 minutes of flight in these conditions, it became clear that there was no way I could pull off any successful photography. I turned around at Hillsville, Virginia, returning along a similar flight path.

Above:

BRP MM 230, Stone Mountain State Park, NC, viewed from the foothills looking northwest toward the Blue Ridge.

Left:

BRP MM 245, Doughton Park, Bluff Mountain, looking east.

The turbulence was continuous and annoying to manage while still in Virginia. My ascent up the Blue Ridge Plateau had been uneventful, so I planned a similar descent. I decided I would get a little closer to the terrain right at the ridgeline—as there were no buildings, vehicles, or people—and I could glide off the ridge into the Piedmont if the engine quit. I was paying close attention as I descended toward the ridgeline to the activity of the trees responding to the wind, and it appeared to be a lee-side area with much quieter conditions.

Upon getting 250 feet past the ridgeline, I encountered a mix of severe turbulence and wind shear unlike anything I thought was possible with flyable wind speeds. The aircraft was almost instantly rolled 110 degrees to the left, partially upside down, while about 300 feet above the ground.

I instantly applied full right aileron and heavy right rudder. The roll rate in a Cub is unimpressive, and my return to proper orientation to the sky was aided by getting rolled harshly 70 degrees to the right, along with vertical turbulence. I hit my head multiple times on the frame above the seat, and gear was flying around the cockpit with a vengeance.

During the violence, I was fighting the airplane like it was a misbehaving fighter jet, using all of the agility I had to control my upper body and keep my vision pointed out the windshield. There was only one quick glance possible at the airspeed indicator, which read 60 miles per

ABOVE:

Yes, there is a canyon in Virginia. BRP MM 180, Dan River descending into the Piedmont, looking north.

LEFT:

BRP MM 180, Dan River valley descending off the Blue Ridge Plateau, looking southwest. Not easily accessible from the BRP.

hour with cruise power in a descent. A brief lull afforded the opportunity to pull the waist belt extremely tight and lower the airplane to maneuvering speed before the next round of vertical turbulence—yet again I managed to bang my head on the ceiling. The accessories in the baggage area that were not secured were getting thrown around, and I used the next calm window to reset the ELT, just in case.

At this point, I thought I was getting away from the turbulence, as I was no longer close to the escarpment. I noted that, in the melee with the wind, I had lost 1,000 feet of altitude, despite being trimmed for cruise. I tightened the waist belt as hard as I could, just in case, even though I thought it was over. One final bang still managed to knock my headset off, and I responded by tightening the shoulder belts as hard as they would go. After a consistent and mild downdraft away from terrain, the wind calmed to 10 knots with sunny skies. My flirt with death quickly became an insultingly idyllic afternoon.

With a 60-minute flight ahead of me, I had plenty of time to think what on earth went wrong with this little charade at the state line. I am familiar with rotors, mountain waves, and downdrafts, and I have never been in a situation this vulnerable. Here, for the second time in my flying career, I was caught in a vulnerable situation—not in epic spires of rock at 14,000 feet, nor the highest peaks over 6,000 feet in North Carolina, but rather at 3,000 feet in the Southeast. (continued page 73)

Above: *BRP MM 170, Rocky Knob Recreation Area, looking northeast.*

PAGE 64: *BRP MM 167, looking northeast.* PAGE 65: *BRP MM 136, looking northeast toward Roanoke.*

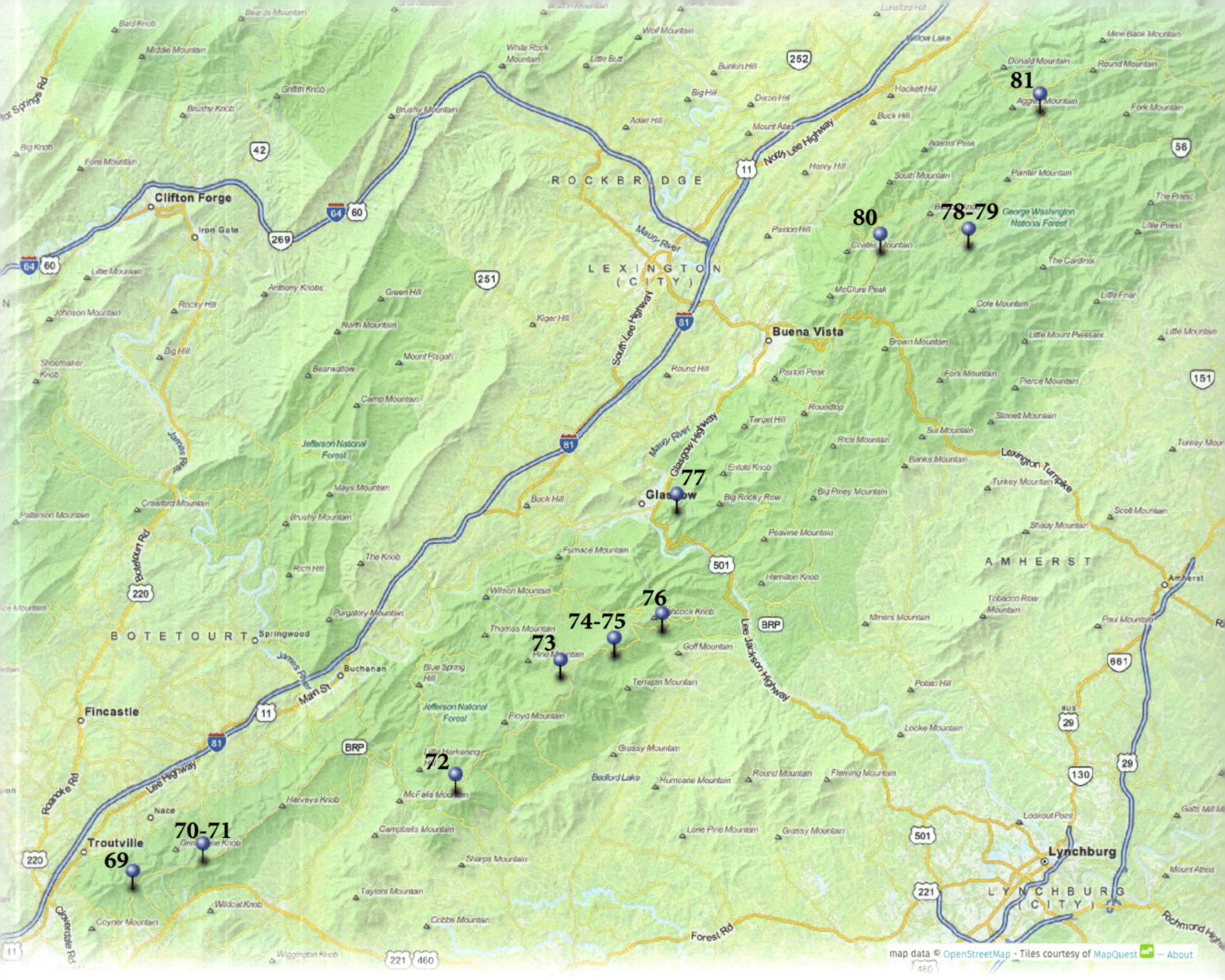

Roanoke to Shenandoah National Park

Page 67:

BRP MM 110, looking northeast.

Pages 70-71:

BRP MM 100, looking northeast toward Blue Knob.

Terrain makes another presence between Roanoke and the northern terminus of the Parkway at Skyline Drive. Once thought to be the highest peaks in North America, the Peaks of Otter, along with a host of other steep mountains rise up off of the Virginia Piedmont, serving also to create the greater Shenandoah Valley, a beautiful region filled with rolling farmland, snaking rivers, and beautiful mountains in all directions. Even driving along I-81, down in the valley, is quite beautiful, and the Parkway takes the high road, looking down below.

While the Parkway ascends to steep peaks with expansive views, it does descend down to the James River, which bisects the Blue Ridge Mountains, and then climbs back up for a period, spending quite a bit of time snaking and twisting through rolling hills.

Right:

BRP MM 104, ascending out of Roanoke VA, looking northeast.

Page 66:

BRP MM 130, looking northeast.

(continued from page 61) The weather phenomenon was not something I expected; it was turbulence and wind shear. My best presumption is one current of air was moving fast over the plateau, and another was stationary in the air mass below over the Piedmont. Two differing airspeeds were most pronounced by the ridgeline, which created a strong shearing force. The reason the windward side did not feature this kind of danger was because of a longer fetch where the two air masses could mix.

I am thankful for three factors that I could control, and which worked in my favor. The first was the fact that I had the bulk of the gear in the aircraft strapped down. Second, I did not follow untrained instinct, which is to pull "up" when rolled

ABOVE:

BRP MM 72, looking east toward descent to James River.

LEFT:

BRP MM 84, ascending from Peaks of Otter to Apple Orchard Mountain, looking northeast.

PAGES 74-75:

BRP MM 68, Blue Ridge Mountains, looking northeast.

over, thanks in part to having read a fine article in *AOPA Pilot* magazine about it in the not too distant past. Being so close to terrain behind me would have been a quick death. The last thing is my personal belief that panic and out-of-control fear has no place in an airplane. While I do not like being turned over, nor do I like getting literally beaten up by the wind, I was still many hundreds of feet from the nearest object. The matter of focus at that moment was not the emotional magnitude of "what if" something worse happens, it was what needed to be done to get out of the situation. An airplane needs to be commanded, and not the other way around.

The most important lesson of the event is to take a cautious approach when getting close to terrain, (continued page 91)

Left:

BRP MM 66, Blue Ridge Mountains with James River Plain, looking northeast.

This Page:

BRP MM 62, west side of Blue Ridge Mountains, looking northeast.

Pages 78-79:

BRP MM 84, looking NW over the Shenandoah Valley.

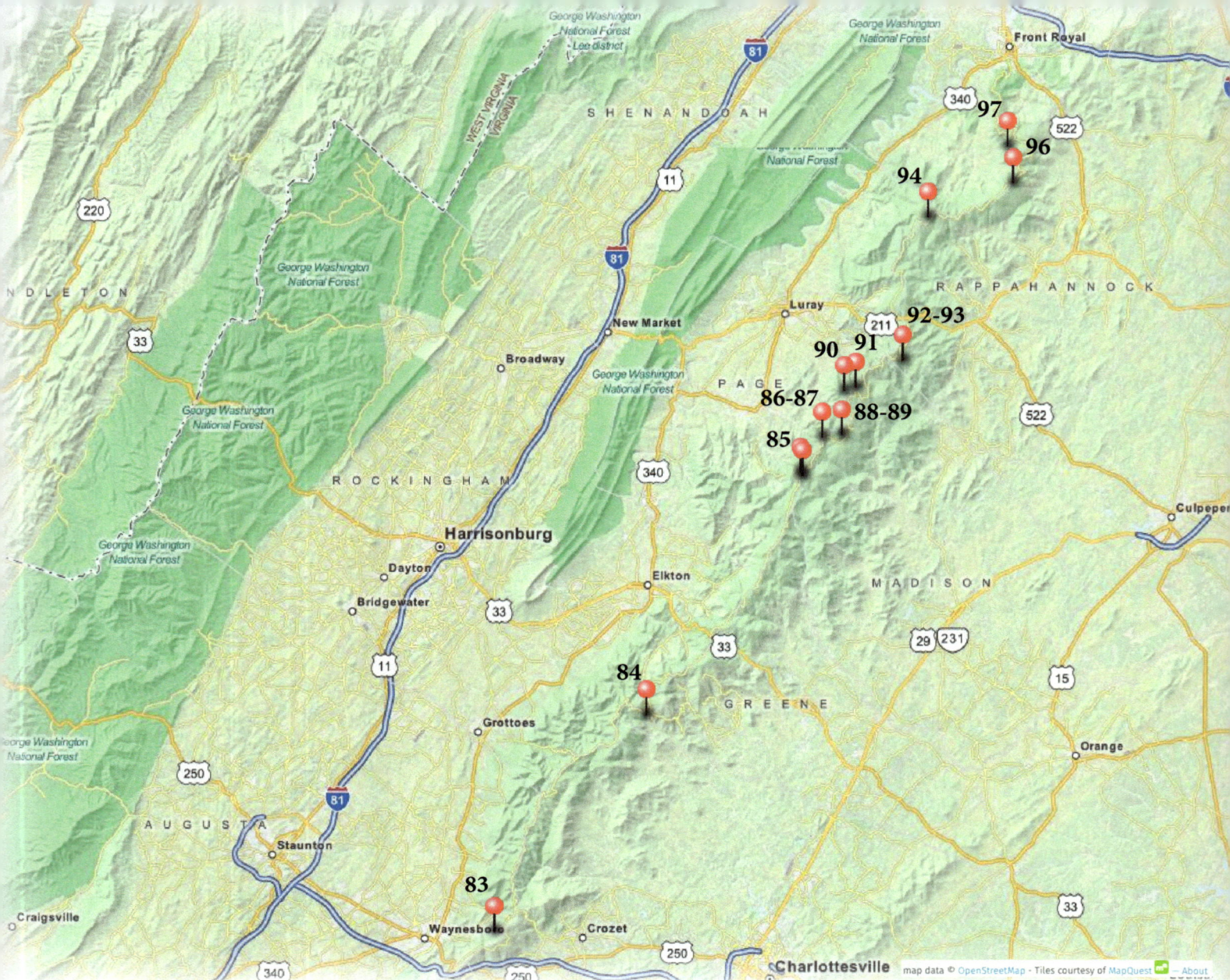

SHENANDOAH NATIONAL PARK

PAGE 84:

Skyline Drive MM 75, looking west toward Massanutten Peak and the Shenandoah Valley.

PAGE 85:

Skyline Drive MM 51, Big Meadows. Top image looking NW, bottom looking E.

I always thought of Skyline Drive merely as an extension of the Blue Ridge Parkway; look at the map and you'll see that the road is a continuation of the same mountain ridgeline as the BRP. It was not until I drove the length of Skyline Drive that I got the point that they are vastly different.

Relatively speaking, the mountain range is quite profound; where views of it from below and views from the summits to the valley are different from the rest of the Appalachians. Instead of a rolling sea of hills, there is a pronounced range, with flat valleys on either side, allowing the magnitude of the mountains to stick out.

This project was the third time I have flown the entire Park: once down low over the farmland, once over the next range over, and this time right down the ridge.

RIGHT:

Skyline Drive MM 99, looking east toward Charlottesville.

PAGE 80:

BRP MM 41, oscillating ridgeline, looking southwest.

PAGE 81:

BRP MM 30, Blue Ridge Mountains overlooking the Shenandoah Valley to the northwest.

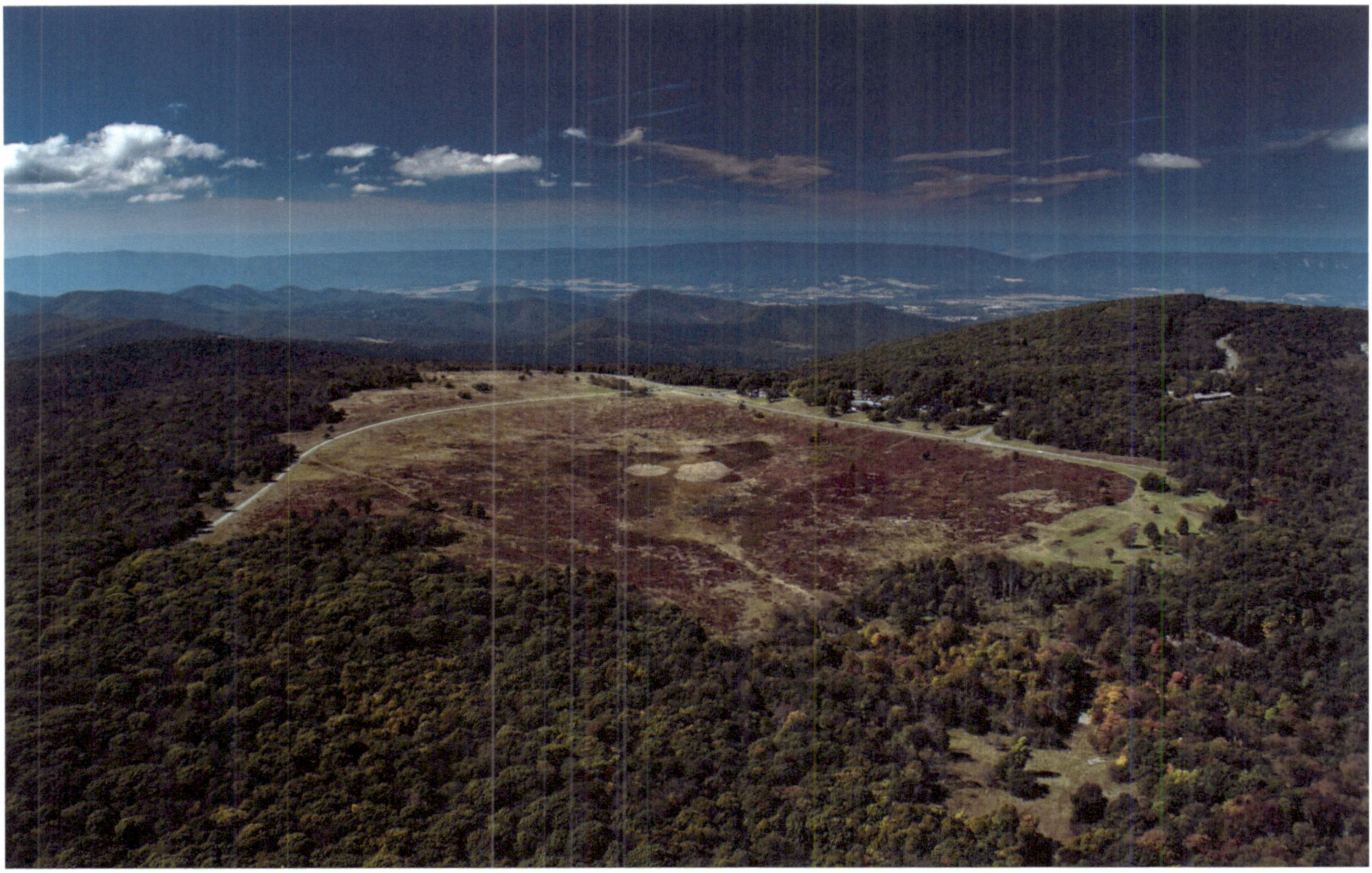

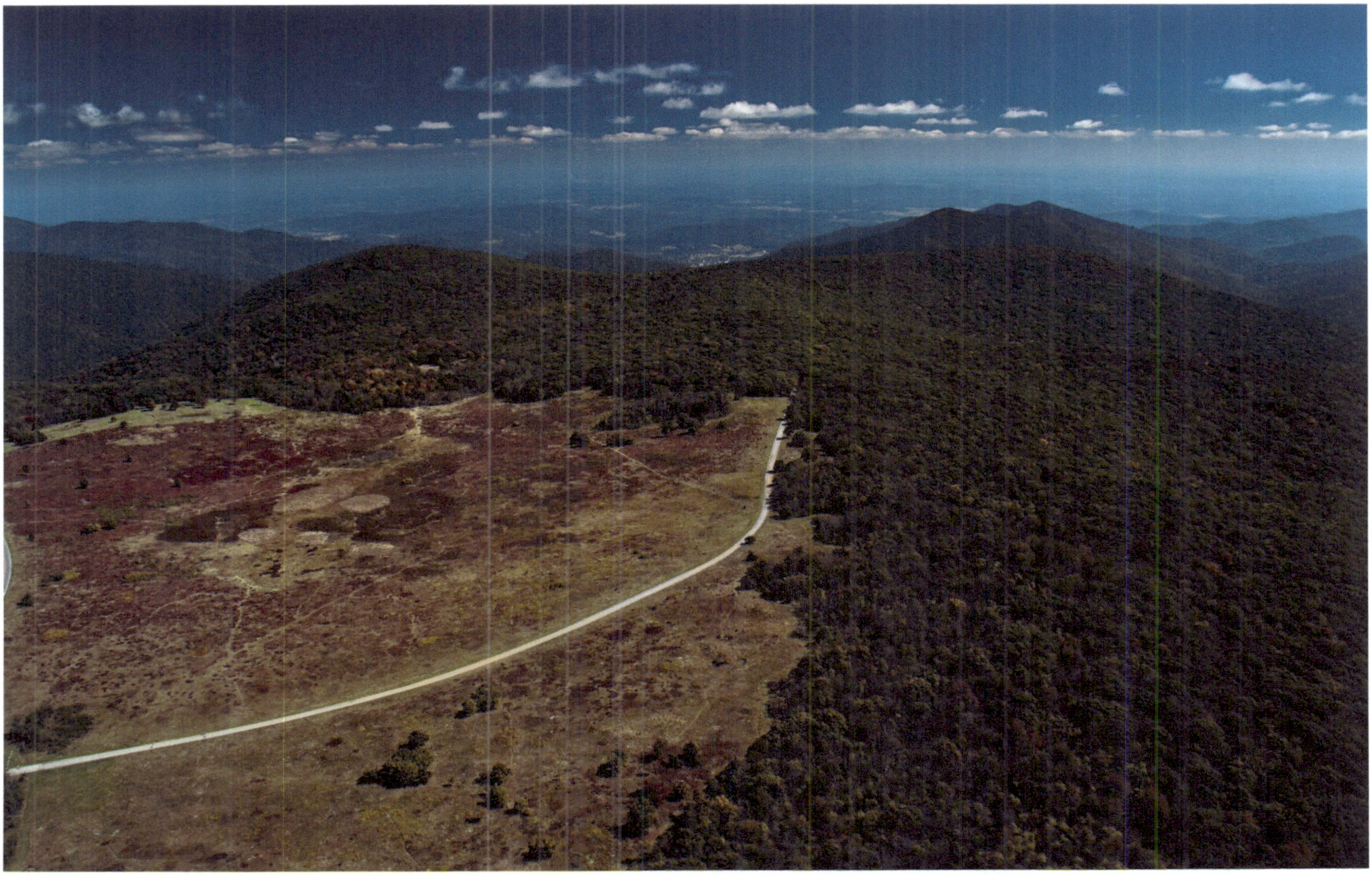

88 **ABOVE:** *Skyline Drive MM 46, Hawksbill (4,051'), highest peak in Shenandoah Nat'l Park, looking northwest.*

PAGES 86-87: *Skyline Drive MM 47, looking east toward Virginia Piedmont.*

(continued from page 73) evaluated daily based on the weather. That's my standard rule, and I ignored it. The second lesson is that terrain is terrain, regardless of how unimpressive the elevations are related to sea level. By thinking I was safe down at 3,000 feet mean sea level, I missed obvious clues and found myself upside down.

PAGES 92-93:

Skyline Drive MM 35 - Stony Man, looking northwest.

ABOVE:

Skyline Drive MM 40 - Stony Man, looking northeast.

LEFT:

Skyline Drive MM 42, near highest point on drive (3,680'), looking northwest over the Shenandoah Valley.

RIGHT:

Found on a hilltop just outside Shenandoah National Park boundaries, this is an example of how often the author finds strange things visible from the air.

ABOVE: *Skyline Drive MM 21, Hogback Mountain, looking east.*

Above: *Skyline Drive MM 8, looking north toward Front Royal.* **Left:** *MM 14, looking southwest.*

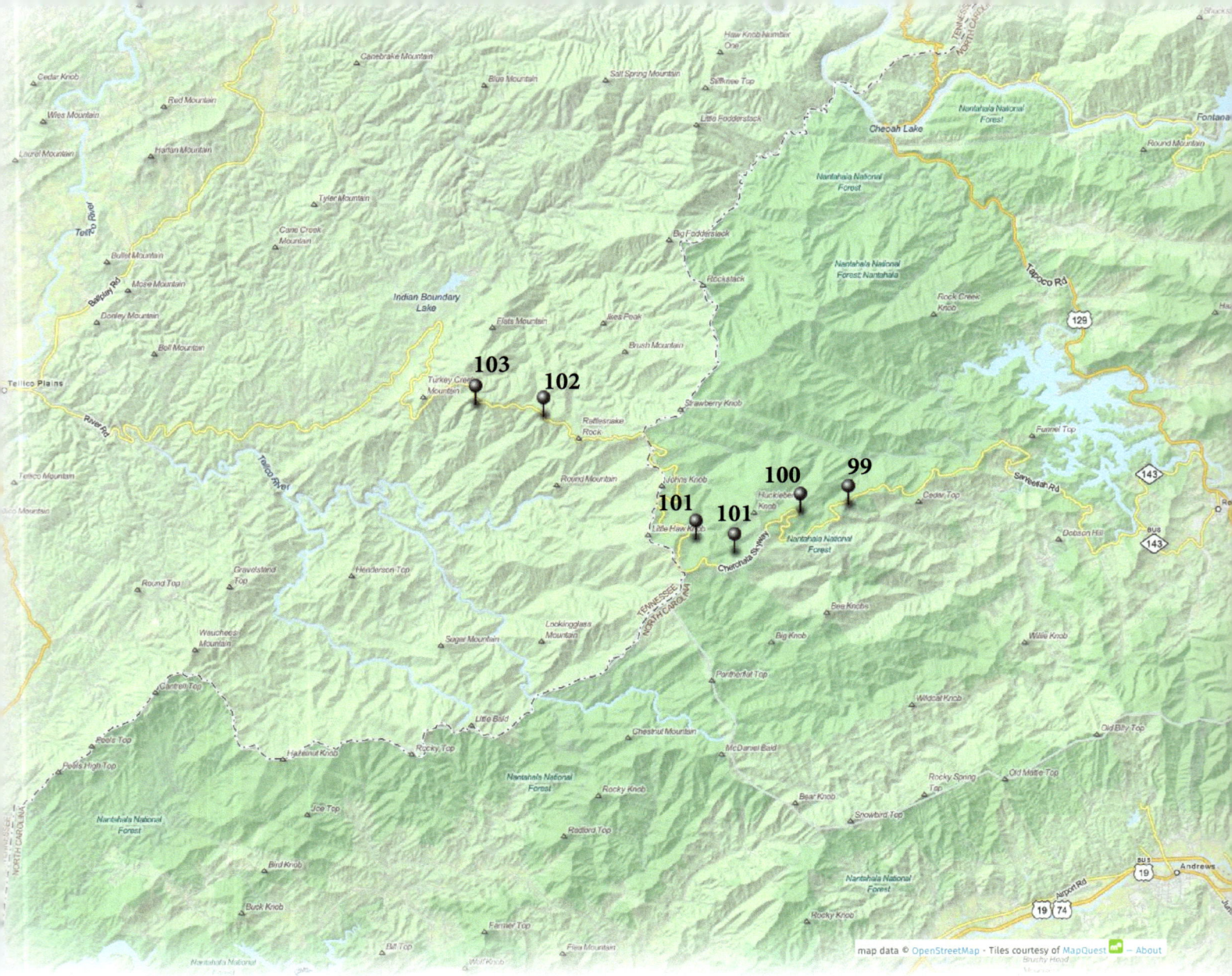

CHEROHALA SKYWAY

PAGE 100:

Cherohala Skyway MM NC 10, looking southwest.

PAGE 101 (TOP):

Cherohala Skyway MM NC 8, looking northeast.

PAGE 101 (BASE):

Cherohala Skyway MM NC 5, looking northwest.

In case you're wondering where Cherohala Skyway fits among the Blue Ridge Parkway and its adjoining cousins, the answer is quite simple: much like the Parkway, Skyline Drive, and US 441, Cherohala Skyway was built as a true parkway where a vehicle is an essential part of the entire experience.

At a cost of $100 million, the road was built expressly for the enjoyment of driving over serious terrain.

There were already other ways to get from one side of the mountain to another, and those involve driving much lower. This road intentionally goes over the top of the mountains to cross the state line.

The parkways of the Appalachians themselves are a work of art, with beautiful curves that hug rolling terrain, emphasizing the graceful curves of an otherwise inhospitable wilderness.

RIGHT:

Cherohala Skyway MM NC 14, looking southwest.

PAGE 102:

Cherohala Skyway MM TN 20, looking west.

PAGE 103:

Cherohala Skyway MM TN 19, looking northwest.

More Books by the Author

Photo Credit: Adam Romer

With a thirst for new and interesting perspectives, Garrett Fisher is perpetually adventure flying, undertaking a variety of projects at any given moment. Currently, he lives on an airpark in Wyoming outside of Yellowstone, where he is working on a host of book projects, two of which will focus on Grand Teton National Park and Yellowstone National Park. He blogs about the flights he takes to explore and document things from the air, providing an abundance of photographs and maps on his website at www.garrettfisher.me.

www.ingramcontent.com/pod-product-compliance
Lightning Source LLC
Chambersburg PA
CBHW042000150426
43194CB00002B/69